learn to knit
at home

It's an enormous privilege to teach a new knitter and to see them grow in skill from their first wobbly stitches to completing their first project and beyond. I can remember my own beginner projects well and how initially I kept forgetting how to purl and couldn't tell which side of stocking stitch was which!

The best way to get good at knitting is to practice lots and try new things. This book contains 14 designs for you and your home using easy stitch patterns and a variety of techniques.

Whether your ambitions are small (tea cosies and mitts) or big (blankets and sweaters) there is a project for you here. Come on in and make yourself at home.

Happy knitting!

Alison

contents

getting started

getting started

HOW TO MAKE A SLIP KNOT

To start your cast on you'll need to make a slip knot:

STEP 1

Make a loop of yarn on the needle as shown in the diagram. The free end is called the 'tail' and the end attached to the ball is the 'working yarn'

STEP 2

Use the point of the needle to pull the working yarn through the loop to make a new loop

STEP 3

Pull the new loop all the way through

STEP 4

Tug the tail and the working yarn to tighten the knot (not too tight though – you'll need to get your other needle through in a minute!)

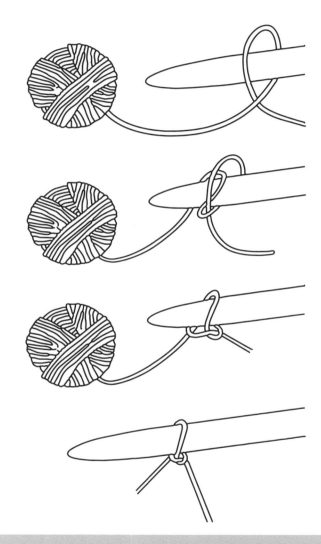

TIP

It's a common beginner problem to cast on too tightly. Practice makes perfect, but if you're finding it difficult to be loose enough, use a bigger needle just for casting on and then swap to the right size for your project for the first row.

baa ram ewe LEARN TO KNIT AT HOME

HOW TO CAST ON ('THUMB' OR 'LONG TAIL' METHOD)

There are lots of different ways to cast on. The thumb or long tail method as shown here is a good choice for most projects.

STEP 1

Start with a slip knot. You will need a long tail, so make sure your tail is about 3 to 4 times the width of the piece you are going to make. The slip knot is your first stitch.

STEP 2

Hold the needle in your right hand and the tail in your left hand

STEP 3

Make a loop over your left thumb as shown in the diagram and put the point of the needle into this loop

STEP 4

Wrap the working yarn around the needle clockwise with your right hand

STEP 5

Pull the working yarn through the loop made in step 3

STEP 6

Pull gently (not too much!) to tighten the stitch

CONTINUE

Repeat steps 3 to 6 to cast on the number of stitches you need.

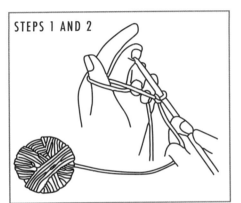

STEPS 1 AND 2

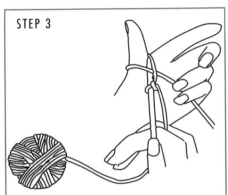

STEP 3

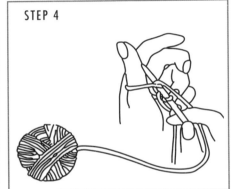

STEP 4

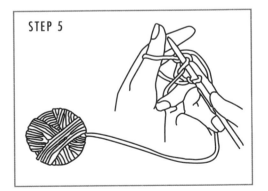

STEP 5

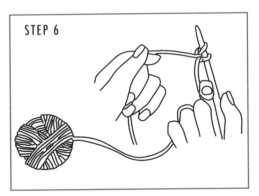

STEP 6

TIP

It's frustrating to run out of yarn in a long tail cast on. You can roughly work out how much yarn you'll need by simply wrapping the yarn around your needle the same number of times as the number of stitches you need to cast on. The yarn you needed to wrap is the length of the tail you will need – easy!

HOW TO DO THE KNIT STITCH

STEP 1
Hold the needle with the cast on stitches in your left hand and the empty needle in your right hand. Put the tip of the right needle into the front leg of the first stitch on the left needle as shown.

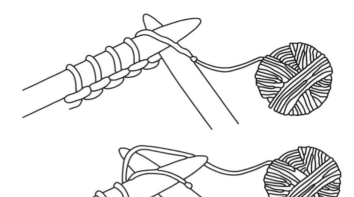

STEP 2
Bring the working yarn (the yarn coming from the ball) under and around the right needle clockwise.

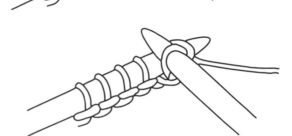

STEP 3
Pull the yarn through to make a loop

STEP 4
Slip the stitch off the left needle, making sure to keep it on the right needle as you do this

CONTINUE
Repeat steps 1 to 4 until all the stitches have been knitted. Then you will have reached the end of the row.
To start the next row, swap the needles over so that the needle with all the stitches is in your left hand and the empty needle is in your right hand.

TIP
It can feel like you need three hands to do everything when you start knitting! Hang in there and you will eventually find your own comfortable position to hold the needles, whether it's wedging the end of the right needle under your arm or holding the right needle with your right hand ring finger and little finger while your thumb and index finger hold the yarn.

TIP
Stitches too tight? Make sure you have the needle pushed into the stitch far enough so you are wrapping the yarn round the needle at the thickest part. If you make your new stitches on the tapered part of the needle at the point you will end up with stitches that will be tight and difficult to move along the needles.

HOW TO DO THE PURL STITCH

STEP 1

Make sure the yarn is in the front of the work. Put the tip of the right needle into the front leg of the first stitch from right to left as shown.

STEP 2

Bring the working yarn around the right needle anti-clockwise

STEP 3

Pull through to make a loop

STEP 4

Slip the stitch off the left needle, making sure to keep it on the right needle as you do this

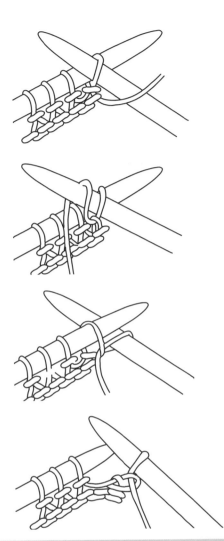

CONTINUE

Repeat steps 1 to 4 until all the stitches have been worked. Then you will have reached the end of the row.

To start the next row, swap the needles over so that the needle with all the stitches is in your left hand and the empty needle is in your right hand.

TIP

When you are doing purl stitches the yarn needs to be in the front of the work. When you are doing knit stitches the yarn needs to be in the back of the work.

If you are switching from knit to purl in the middle of the row, take the yarn between the needles from the back to the front before you begin the stitch.

If you are switching from purl to knit in the middle of the row, take the yarn between the needles from the front to the back before you begin the stitch.

It's a common beginner mistake to put the needle in the next stitch and then move the yarn. If you do that you will end up with extra loops on the needle.

HOW TO CAST OFF

STEP 1
Knit two stitches as normal, then use the point of the left needle to pick up the first stitch and pull it over the second stitch and off the right needle.

STEP 2
Knit the next stitch as normal and then pick up the rightmost stitch on the right needle and pull it over the leftmost stitch.

STEP 3
Repeat step 2 until all the stitches on the left needle have been worked. There will be one stitch left on the right needle. Cut the yarn and pull it all the way through the last stitch.

> **TIP**
> *When you cut the yarn, leave at least 15cm (6") as a tail to sew in. Tiny, short tails are very fiddly when you come to sew the ends in!*

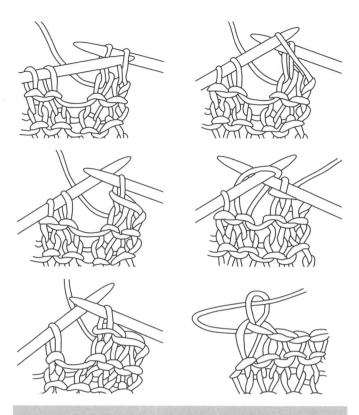

> **TIP**
> *Some people find their cast offs can be very tight. This can be a problem if the edge needs to stretch to fit over a hand, foot or head. An easy way to make a looser cast off is to use a bigger needle for the right needle. It can also help to relax and not rush the cast off. This a problem often suffered by knitters who hurry the last stitches!*

HOW TO CAST OFF IN PATTERN

If the pattern tells you to 'cast off in pattern', you should work the cast off row using the same stitch pattern used in the rows below. When you come to the next stitch on the left needle, knit or purl it according to the stitch pattern before casting it off.

HOW TO DECREASE (KNIT TWO TOGETHER OR K2TOG)
There are lots of different ways to decrease in knitting. This is the easiest one, called 'knit two together' and written in patterns as **k2tog**.

STEP 1
Put the right needle into the front of the next **two** stitches on the left needle.

STEP 2
Bring the yarn around the needle and knit the stitch as normal

STEP 3
Slip the two stitches off the left hand needle together

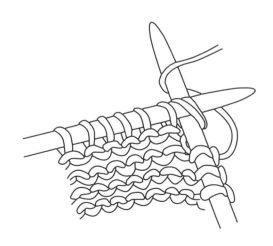

HOW TO INCREASE (KNIT FRONT AND BACK OR KFB)

There are many kinds of increases in knitting. This is one easy way known as 'knit front and back' because you knit into the front and back leg of the same stitch. It's written in patterns as **kfb**.

STEP 1

Knit the stitch as normal but **do not slip the old stitch off the left needle**

STEP 2

Keeping the partially worked stitch on the right needle, put the point of the right needle into the **back leg** of the stitch on the left needle

STEP 3

Knit the stitch through the back leg, then drop the old stitch off the left needle as normal.

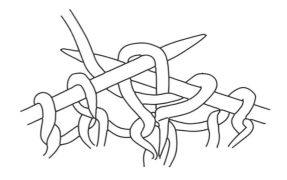

TIP

Why do you have to knit through the back leg? Well, if you try to knit twice through the front leg you'll soon see it won't work and you'll just end up undoing your first stitch! But if you like you can knit and then purl into the front leg for an increase that works just as well as kfb.

HOW TO JOIN NEW YARN AND CHANGE COLOUR

If your ball of yarn runs out or if you want to knit a stripe, you will need to join a new ball.

The easiest way to do this is at the beginning of a new row.

All you have to do is start knitting the new row using the new ball of yarn. Make sure you leave a long enough tail (about 15cm or 6") to sew in at the end.

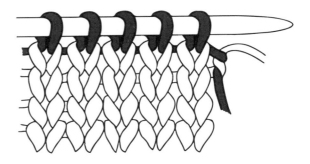

To stop the edge stitches being loose you can tie the ends together when you have knitted a few stitches in the new yarn.

If you are working a very long row and the ball runs out, in a big blanket for example, you can join new yarn by just knitting the next stitch with the new ball. Tie the ends together loosely after a few stitches. You will need to untie them and weave in the ends when you finish.

SEWING UP

Sewing up neatly really makes a big difference to your projects. It can be tempting to rush the sewing up if you are in a hurry to finish up and use your project. But it's better to do it carefully and if something doesn't look quite right, undo your sewing and try again.

MATTRESS STITCHES

Mattress stitch is the neatest way to finish a vertical seam and if it's done well it's invisible from the right side. Many of the projects in this book can be sewn up using mattress stitch for stocking stitch – even if they are ribbed, the edge stitches are in stocking stitch and can be sewn using this method.

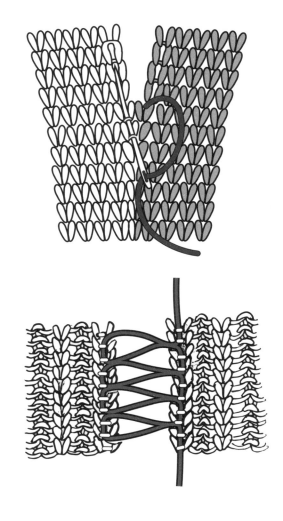

MATTRESS STITCH FOR SEWING UP STOCKING STITCH

Make sure the right sides are facing towards you. If they are two separate pieces, lay them down flat. Bring the edges to be sewn up together and line them up at the top and bottom.

Thread a tapestry needle with yarn and insert it half a stitch in from the edge on the first row on one piece. You will be catching the horizontal bar of yarn with the tapestry needle. Take the tapestry needle across to the first row on the other piece and insert it into half a stitch in from the edge, again catching the horizontal bar.

Insert the needle in the second row half a stitch in from the edge on one piece and then in same place on the second row in the other piece.
Keep going from one side to the other in a zig zag until you have worked all the rows.

MATTRESS STITCH FOR OTHER STITCH PATTERNS

This is worked in a similar way to stocking stitch, but you will need to go in one whole stitch from each edge

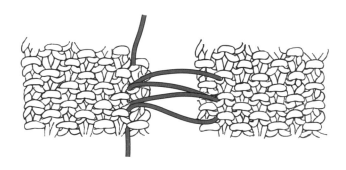

TIPS
Make sure you match the pieces all the way up – check as you go along that you aren't using up one side faster than the other. You can work loosely to start with and then tighten up by pulling gently on the yarn after a few rows have been worked Try to insert the tapestry needle in the same column all the way up the seam as this will give the neatest result.

WHIPSTITCH

Whipstitch makes a strong but bulky seam which is useful for small pieces like stuffed toy parts where the inside of the seam doesn't need to be smooth. To whipstitch, hold the pieces with right sides touching and wrong sides out.

STEP 1

Thread a tapestry needle and use it to sew from front to back through the pieces close to the edge

STEP 2

Bring the yarn over the top of the edge and then sew from front to back through the pieces.

Repeat step 2 across the edge to be seamed.

HOW TO SEW IN ENDS

The easiest place to sew in ends is in the seams. You can do this if you always changed to a new ball of yarn at the beginning of a row and your piece is sewn up.

If you have ends that can't be sewn into seams, you can sew them in on the back of the work. Weave them up and down through the stitches on the back for 2-3cm (1"). Then snip the remaining yarn off close to the surface.

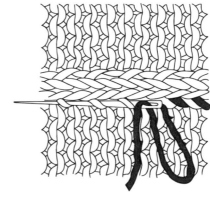

BUTTON LOOP

STEP 1

Thread a tapestry needle with yarn. Bring the yarn through the edge of the knitting, leaving a short end. Go back down through the knitting leaving a loop big enough to fit over the button. Repeat this until you have three or four loops the same size.

STEP 2

Sew as shown over all the loops to reinforce the button loop.

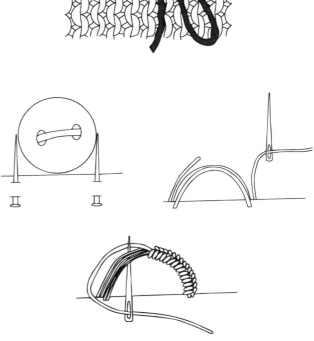

POM POM

STEP 1
Cut two cardboard circles the same size as the pom pom. Cut a hole in the middle of each circle.

STEP 2
Holding the two pieces of card together, wrap yarn around the circles until the hole in the middle is full.

STEP 3
Cut the yarn between the two circles of card.

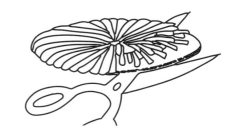

STEP 4
Pull the circles apart and tie a long length of yarn around the middle of the bunch of yarn, making sure to knot the yarn tightly

STEP 5
Remove the cards and trim the pom pom to neaten it.

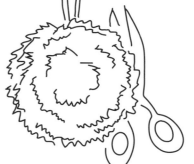

RIGHT SIDE AND WRONG SIDE

In a pattern you'll sometimes see the abbreviations "RS" and "WS". These are short for Right Side and Wrong Side. The right side is the front of the piece, which will be visible when it is in use. The wrong side is the back, which is not usually seen when the piece is in use.

When you're a beginner you might find it more difficult to tell apart the right and wrong sides. You can pin a safety pin or locking stitch marker to the right side so you can tell them apart. (This is also a good idea if you ever knit in fluffy yarn when even experienced knitters can find it hard to tell which side is which.)

Each stitch pattern is a bit different when it comes to right and wrong sides.

Garter stitch looks the same on both sides. You will probably find that the cast on and cast off edges look a bit neater on one side than the other so you can pick the best side to be the right side when you sew up. If you change colour in garter stitch there will be a right side and wrong side – you'll be able to tell because the colour change will look neater on one side than the other.

Stocking stitch looks very different on each side. The right side looks like columns of little 'V's and the wrong side looks like rows of bumps. The side with rows of bumps is reverse stocking stitch and can be used as a stitch pattern in its own right.

Welted patterns look almost the same on each side. The bottom and top edges will look different, as one side will start with stocking stitch and on the other side it will start with reverse stocking stitch. In this book the right side will always begin with reverse stocking stitch because it naturally curls under and looks neater.

Ribbed patterns look similar on each side, but this time it's the edge stitches that will look different. Check the pattern to see which side is the right and wrong side and mark it if you need to.

GAUGE

Gauge, also known as tension, is all about how tightly or loosely you knit. Patterns usually give the required gauge in the introduction and you need to match that gauge for a successful project.

WHY DOES GAUGE MATTER?

1. It affects the finished size of your item. Knit too loosely, and your project will come out bigger than the size given in the pattern. Knit too tightly, and your project will come out smaller.
2. If you don't knit to gauge, you may use more yarn than the pattern states and so you could run out.
3. Gauge affects the finished fabric you make. Knit too loosely and your item may be holey and floppy. Knit too tightly and your item might end up feeling like cardboard! Sometimes knitting more tightly (in the case of snug fitting ribbed items) or loosely (in the case of scarves and shawls) than usual for the yarn is desirable and the gauge given in the pattern will take this into account.

HOW TO GET THE RIGHT GAUGE

For most projects, you need to check your gauge before you cast on (the exception would be very small items, like the mug cosies and bunting triangles in this book, where your swatch would actually be bigger than the project itself!).

To check your gauge, you need to make a swatch, which is a square-ish piece of knitting about 15cm x 15cm (6" x 6"). It's important your swatch is not smaller than this so that you can measure accurately. Make sure you are using the same needles you plan to knit your project with and the same yarn, as both needles and yarn affect your finished gauge. The yarn amount given in the pattern will include enough to make a swatch.

To get an idea of how many stitches to cast on for about the right size for your swatch, take the first number in the gauge printed (e.g. "18 stitches") and cast on about one and a half times that number. It doesn't have to be exact. Then, knit in the stitch pattern listed with the gauge until the piece measures about 15cm (6") from the cast on edge. Cast off.

The next step is really important – you need to block your swatch. Some yarns can change in gauge after washing, so you could end up with a nasty surprise when you wash your project for the first time if you skip this step. Follow the instructions given for blocking on page 17.

Now it's time to measure and check your stitch gauge. Lay your swatch out flat and measure 10cm (4") across the width in the middle of the piece (not too close to the edges) and mark each end with a pin. Count the number of stitches between the pins and compare to the gauge given in the pattern.

If you have the same number of stitches to 10cm (4"), then your stitch gauge is perfect.
If you have more stitches to 10cm (4") then you are knitting too tightly and you will need to use a bigger needle.
If you have fewer stitches to 10cm (4") then you are knitting too loosely and you will need to use a smaller needle.

You also need to check the row gauge. Measure 10cm (4") vertically on your swatch and mark with pins, then count and compare.

If you need to change needle size, knit another swatch and repeat the process. Try one needle size smaller or bigger to start with, as that can often be all you need.

Changing needle size will affect both stitch gauge and row gauge. Usually you should try to get your stitch gauge perfect, and if your row gauge is a little different your project will still be fine – it's quite normal for knitters to match stitch gauge but not row gauge.

SPECIAL RULES FOR SWATCHING DIFFERENT STITCH PATTERNS

For **Stocking stitch**, you should start by working a few rows of garter stitch (knit every row). About 6 rows is enough. Then, work the first and last few stitches of the row in garter stitch. That means that you need to knit all the right side rows and on the wrong side work this row:

K3, purl to last 3 stitches, k3.

You need to do this because stocking stitch on its own naturally curls up. Making a garter stitch border on your swatch will make it easier to measure.

For **ribbed** projects there are two things to be aware of:
You need to cast on the right number of stitches. The pattern will be given in the gauge as something like "2x2 rib". This means that the rib is worked as two knit stitches followed by two purl stitches. Add both numbers together and make sure you cast on a multiple of this number for your swatch. So, for example, for 2x2 rib you would need to cast on a multiple of 4.

The gauge in rib is often quite different from the stocking stitch gauge. This is because rib can be very stretchy (and the smaller the numbers in the rib pattern, the stretchier it is – so 2x2 rib is much more stretchy than 6x6 rib). The purl stitches in a tightly knitted rib 'hide' between the knit stitches until you stretch it out and they become visible. The gauge may be given for both stretched and unstretched rib and you should check both.

YARN

All the projects in this book use baa ram ewe Dovestone Natural Aran and Dovestone Natural Chunky. These lovely yarns are made from 100% British wool, processed and spun entirely in Yorkshire and blended from natural coloured sheep fleeces to create a palette of five shades.

Using good quality yarn will make a big difference to your finished projects – they'll drape better and feel more snuggly. Wool is very forgiving and can be pulled out and re-knitted lots of times. It's also breathable and warm, as well as being a renewable fibre.

Before you start, make sure you read the yarn label, as it will tell you lots of important information, including the suggested gauge (see page 15 for more information about gauge), washing instructions and the number of metres/yards per ball or skein.

Yarns come in various weights shown in the table below. The two used in this book are called 'aran' (also known as 'worsted') and 'chunky' (also known as 'bulky').

Thinnest	2ply, 3ply and lace weight
	4ply / *fingering*
	Sport weight
	Double Knitting or DK
	Aran / *worsted*
	Chunky / *bulky*
Thickest	Super chunky / *super bulky*

(Weight names used mostly in North America are in italics)

In case you want to substitute for a different yarn, here are the key facts:

Dovestone Natural Aran: aran/worsted weight, 100% wool, 170 metres/186 yards per 100g skein, suggested gauge 18 sts to 10cm/4"

Dovestone Natural Chunky: chunky/bulky weight, 100% wool, 120 metres /131 yards per 100g ball, suggested gauge 14 sts to 10cm/4"

When substituting yarn, look for one that has the same suggested gauge, and make sure you calculate how much you need by the total number of metres or yards for your project – don't assume all balls or skeins are the same length – they are just the same weight!

If you are using a yarn that comes in a twisted skein (also called a hank), you will need to make it into a ball before you knit with it (don't do what my friend did – she skipped this step and started knitting, and ended up with a massive tangle!). Start by taking the label off and popping the end of the skein out and undoing the twist so you have a big loop. Find a friend to hold the yarn for you or put it over the back of a chair to keep the loop open. Look for any ties and undo them or carefully snip the knots off. One of the knots will include the ends of the yarn – start winding with one of these. Once it's wound into a ball you can begin knitting with it.

If you want to know more about yarn, *The Knitter's Book of Yarn* by Clara Parkes is a great place to start.

NEEDLES

Knitting needles come in different sizes and different materials. The size you need will depend on the yarn and pattern but it's your choice whether you use wood, plastic or metal (or even the more exotic types like carbon fibre or glass).

Straight needles are the type of needles most people have seen before. They come in pairs and each needle has a point on one end and a knob on the other end so stitches can't come off that end.

Circular needles are made with two points joined by a flexible cable. They are useful for knitting large pieces like blankets that are made in one piece and are required for a few projects in this book where it would be impossible to fit all the stitches onto a straight needle. Some people find circular needles are easier on their hands and wrists because they are less heavy and the weight of the project can sit in your lap rather than dangle from the needles.

You might also see short straight needles with points at both ends. These are double pointed needles (DPNs) and are meant for knitting in the round. None of the projects in this book use DPNs.

BLOCKING

Blocking simply means finishing the fabric you have made. Blocking helps to even out wobbly stitches and wonky edges and makes your knitting look much more professional. It also makes sewing up much easier.

The simplest kind of blocking is just washing your knitting.

Here's how to wash your hand-knit woollens:
1. Fill a sink or bucket with warm water.
2. Add wool or delicates wash, mix gently (you don't want soap suds) and your knitting. Check the label on the bottle of wool wash for how much to add.
3. Lift your knitting out, being careful not to stretch it. Empty the sink or bucket.
4. Fill with cold water and rinse out your knitting (some wool washes don't need to be rinsed out. Check the label to see). Repeat if needed.
5. Take your knitting out and lay it on a towel. Place another towel on top and roll up into a sausage shape. Gently squeeze the towels to remove as much excess water as possible.
6. Unroll the towels and lay your knitting flat to dry. If the pattern gives dimensions for the finished pieces, make sure you lay it out to the right measurements.

Looking after your knitting when you wash it
- don't agitate it, rub it or scrub at it. This is exactly what you do to make felt so you shouldn't do it to your knitting unless you want it to shrink!
- don't wring it out or stretch it as you take it out of the water
- don't dunk straight from hot water to cold or vice versa. Hot water is actually fine for wool (though not so good for dye, as hot water can make dye come off fibres) but 'shocking' it with a sudden change in temperature can lead to felting and shrinking

MORE ADVANCED BLOCKING

Some patterns will specify pressing or pinning out to size, because the stitch pattern needs some extra help to get it into the shape needed. Knitting is very good at being prodded and poked into shape! If you pin out your knitting when it's wet and let it dry fully it will keep that shape. You can pin into a thick towel over a carpet or rug, but many knitters like to use interlocking foam mats.

Pressing can help to flatten a bouncy stitch pattern that needs to lie flat. If this is needed then the pattern will specify it.

If you are using a synthetic yarn, steam blocking works best. Dampen your knitting with a spray bottle and hold a steam iron over it (be careful not to touch the knitting or steam it too heavily as you could melt or denature the yarn).

Remember that you can (and should!) practice blocking with your gauge swatch.

baa ram ewe LEARN TO KNIT AT HOME

sid mug cosies

Why should teapots have all the cosies? Mug cosies are quick to knit and very easy – perfect for practising your stitches. Choose from five different stitch patterns: garter stitch, stocking stitch, moss stitch, ribbed and welted.

YARN
Dovestone Natural Aran.
Each mug cosy will need about 35m/38yds of yarn

NEEDLES
5mm (US 8) and 4.5mm (US 7) straight needles.
Small buttons, about 15mm (½") diameter.

GAUGE
Exact gauge is not required with these mug cosies.

ABBREVIATIONS
A list of standard abbreviations appears on the inside back cover.

FINISHED SIZE
All the mug cosies are rectangles, approx 7 to 8cm (2¾" to 3") on the short edge. They are made to fit a mug of 25.5cm (10") circumference; the length depends on the stitch pattern. Stocking stitch and moss stitch cosies are made to fit the mug exactly. Welted, ribbed and garter stitch cosies are intended to stretch to fit.

The ribbed mug cosy is knit from the bottom up (which means you cast on for the long edge) and the other mug cosies are all knitted sideways (which means you cast on for the short edge).

GARTER STITCH MUG COSY
(shown in shade 8)

Using 5mm (US 8) needles, cast on 15 stitches.

Knit every row until piece measures 24cm (9½").
Cast off.

FINISHING
Block following instructions on page 17. Use the yarn tails to sew the bottom two cast on and cast off stitches and the top two stitches together. This makes the hole for the mug handle. You can sew more stitches if you need to fit your mug handle.

Weave in all ends.

STOCKING STITCH MUG COSY
(shown in shade 6)

Using 5mm (US 8) needles, cast on 15 stitches.

Row 1 (RS): Knit.
Row 2 (WS): Knit.
Rows 3-5: Knit.
Row 6: K2, purl to last 2 stitches, k2.
Row 7: Knit
Repeat rows 6-7 until piece measures 25cm (10").
Rows 8-10: Knit.
Cast off.

FINISHING

A small piece of stocking stitch with narrow garter stitch borders like this mug cosy has a tendency to curl. You can solve this in blocking, by dampening it lightly and pressing gently with a steam iron on medium heat to flatten it. If you choose to substitute yarn and use one made from synthetic fibres, be careful not to melt the yarn!

Use the yarn tails to sew the bottom two cast on and cast off stitches together. Sew a button on one side of the top of the mug cosy and make a button loop (see page 11) on the other side.

Weave in all ends.

MOSS STITCH MUG COSY
(shown in shade 4)

Using 5mm (US 8) needles, cast on 15 stitches.

Row 1: K1, *p1, k1; repeat from * to end of row.
Repeat this row until piece measures 24cm (9½").
Cast off.

FINISHING
Block following instructions on page 17. Complete sewing and fastenings as for Stocking Stitch mug cosy.

WELTED MUG COSY
(shown in shade 2)

Using 5mm (US 8) needles, cast on 15 stitches.

Row 1 (RS): Purl.
Row 2 (WS): Knit.
Row 3: Purl.
Row 4: Knit.

Row 5: Knit.
Row 6: Purl.
Row 7: Knit.
Row 8: Purl.

Repeat rows 1-8 eight more times.

Row 9: Purl.
Row 10: Knit.
Row 11: Purl.
Row 12: Knit.

Cast off.
Finish as for Garter Stitch mug cosy.

RIBBED MUG COSY
(shown in shade 5)

Using 4.5mm (US 7) needles, cast on 50 stitches.

Row 1 (RS): K2, *p2, k2; repeat from * to end of row.
Row 2 (WS): P2, *k2, p2; repeat from * to end of row.

Repeat rows 1-2 until mug cosy measures 8cm (3") from cast on edge.

Cast off.

FINISHING
Block following instructions on page 17. Use the yarn tails to sew the bottom two stitches on the short edges together and the top two stitches on the short edges together.

Weave in all ends.

wesley bunting

Bunting is great for practising increasing and decreasing. There are five different stitch patterns for you to have a go at. Mix and match colours and stitch patterns across your bunting however you like – you could make a string of bunting in just one stitch pattern in lots of colours, or use just one colour in several stitch patterns.

YARN
Dovestone Natural Chunky. Each bunting triangle needs about 20m/22 yds of yarn.

NEEDLES
6mm (US 10) and 6.5mm (US 10.5) straight needles. Ribbon; Sewing thread and sewing needle

SPECIAL INSTRUCTIONS
K3tog is worked just like k2tog – place your right needle into the next three stitches and knit them together as one stitch.

GAUGE
The gauge for each triangle is given with each stitch pattern. Because these are very small pieces you probably won't want to knit a gauge square – instead, knit one triangle in your chosen stitch pattern and treat it as your gauge piece.
Exact gauge isn't important but if your gauge is very different your triangles will come out at different sizes. Small differences in finished size can be dealt with in blocking. You may need to change needle size to obtain the right gauge.

ABBREVIATIONS
A list of standard abbreviations appears on the inside back cover.

FINISHED SIZE
All the triangles should measure approximately 16cm (6¼") wide across the top and 15cm (6") tall from the bottom point to the middle of the top. You will need to block the triangles to size (see finishing instructions below).

GARTER STITCH BUNTING TRIANGLE

GAUGE
14 stitches x 24 rows = 10cm/4" on 6.5mm needles in garter stitch after blocking

The garter stitch triangle is worked from the bottom point upwards. It's easy to make a bigger triangle if you want, just keep repeating rows 11-14.

Using 6.5mm needles, cast on 1 stitch.

Row 1: Kfb. (There will now be 2 stitches)
Row 2: Kfb, k1. (3 stitches)
Rows 3-4: Knit 2 rows.

Row 5: Kfb, k2. (4 stitches)
Row 6: K1, kfb, k2. (5 stitches)
Rows 7-8: Knit 2 rows.

Row 9: K1, kfb, k3. (6 stitches)
Row 10: K1, kfb, k4. (7 stitches)
Rows 11-12: Knit 2 rows.
Row 13: K1, kfb, knit to end. (8 stitches)
Row 14: K1, kfb, knit to end. (9 stitches)
Repeat rows 11-14 until there are 23 stitches.
Knit 2 rows.
Cast off.

Weave in ends.

STOCKING STITCH BUNTING TRIANGLE

GAUGE
14 stitches x 20 rows = 10cm/4" on 6.5mm needles in stocking stitch after blocking

The stocking stitch triangle is worked from the top downwards.

Using 6.5mm needles, cast on 23 stitches.
Row 1 (RS): Knit.
Row 2 (WS): Knit.
Rows 3-5: Knit.

Row 6: K3, purl to last 3 stitches, k3.
Row 7: K3, k2tog, knit to last 5 stitches, k2tog, k3. (There will now be 21 stitches)
Repeat rows 6 and 7 until 9 stitches remain.

Row 8: K3, p3, k3.
Row 9: K3, k3tog, k3. (7 stitches)
Row 10: Knit.
Row 11: K1, k2tog, knit to end. (6 stitches)
Row 12: Repeat row 11. (5 stitches)
Rows 13-14: Knit.
Row 15: K2tog, knit to end. (4 stitches)
Row 16: K2tog, knit to end. (3 stitches)
Row 17: Knit.
Row 18: K2tog, k1. (2 stitches)
Row 19: K2tog. (1 stitch)
Break yarn and pull through remaining stitch.

Weave in ends.

RIBBED BUNTING

GAUGE
19 stitches x 22 rows = 10cm/4" on 6mm needles in 3x3 rib after blocking and pressing

The ribbed triangle is worked from the top downwards.

Using 6mm needles, cast on 31 stitches.

Row 1 (RS): K1, p1, [k3, p3] four times, k3, p1, k1.
Row 2 (WS): P1, k1, [p3, k3] four times, p3, k1, p1.
Row 3: K2tog, [k3, p3] four times, k3, k2tog. (There will now be 29 stitches)
Row 4: P4, [k3, p3] three times, k3, p4.
Row 5: K2tog, k2, [p3, k3] three times, p3, k2, k2tog. (27 stitches)
Row 6: [P3, k3] four times, p3.
Row 7: K2tog, k1, [p3, k3] three times, p3, k1, k2tog. (25 stitches)

Row 8: P2, [k3, p3] three times, k3, p2.
Row 9: K2tog, [p3, k3] three times, p3, k2tog. (23 stitches)
Row 10: P2, k2, [p3, k3] twice, p3, k2, p2.
Row 11: K2tog, p2, [k3, p3] twice, k3, p2, k2tog. (21 stitches)
Row 12: P2, k1, [p3, k3] twice, p3, k1, p2.
Row 13: K2tog, p1, [k3, p3] twice, k3, p1, k2tog. (19 stitches)
Row 14: P5, k3, p3, k3, p5.
Row 15: K2tog, [k3, p3] twice, k3, k2tog. (17 stitches)
Row 16: P4, k3, p3, k3, p4.
Row 17: K2tog, k2, p3, k3, p3, k2, k2tog. (15 stitches)
Row 18: [P3, k3] twice, p3.
Row 19: K2tog, k1, p3, k3, p3, k1, k2tog. (13 stitches)
Row 20: P2, k3, p3, k3, p2.
Row 21: K2tog, p3, k3, p3, k2tog. (11 stitches)
Row 22: P2, k2, p3, k2, p2.
Row 23: K2tog, p2, k3, p2, k2tog. (9 stitches)
Row 24: P2, k1, p3, k1, p2.
Row 25: K2tog, p1, k3, p1, k2tog. (7 stitches)
Row 26: Purl.
Row 27: K2tog, k3, k2tog. (5 stitches)
Row 28: Purl.
Row 29: K2tog, k1, k2tog. (3 stitches)
Row 30: Purl.
Row 31: K3tog. (1 stitch)

Break yarn and pull through remaining stitch.

Weave in ends.

WELTED BUNTING

GAUGE
13 stitches x 24 rows = 10cm/4" on 6.5mm needles in welted pattern after blocking and pressing

The welted triangle is worked from the top downwards. The welted pattern creates ridges of stocking stitch and reverse stocking stitch. If you lose count of your rows, check the reverse stocking stitch side where you can easily count your rows. Every welted ridge is four rows deep.

Using 6.5mm needles, cast on 21 stitches.

Row 1: Purl.
Row 2: Knit.
Row 3: Purl.
Row 4: Knit.
Row 5: K1, k2tog, knit to last 3 stitches, k2tog, k1. (There will now be 19 stitches)
Row 6: Purl.
Row 7: K1, k2tog, knit to last 3 stitches, k2tog, k1. (17 stitches)
Row 8: Purl.

Repeat these 8 rows until 5 stitches remain, ending after you have worked 32 rows in total.

Row 9: Purl.
Row 10: Knit.
Row 11: Purl.
Row 12: Knit.
Row 13: K2tog, k1, k2tog. (3 stitches)
Row 14: Purl.
Row 15: K3tog. (1 stitch)

Break yarn and pull through remaining stitch.

Weave in ends.

MOSS STITCH BUNTING

NOTE:
This stitch pattern is called moss stitch in the UK. In the USA it is known as seed stitch.

GAUGE
14 stitches x 25 rows = 10cm/4" on 6.5mm needles in moss stitch after blocking

The moss stitch triangle is worked from the top downward.

Using 6.5mm needles, cast on 23 stitches.

Row 1: *K1, p1; repeat from * to last stitch, k1.
Repeat this row three more times.

Row 2: K2tog, *k1, p1; repeat from * to last 3 stitches, k1, k2tog. (There will now be 21 stitches)
Row 3: *P1, k1; repeat from * to last stitch, p1.

Row 4: K1, *k1, p1; repeat from * to last 2 stitches, k2.
Row 5: *P1, k1; repeat from * to last stitch, p1.
Row 6: K2tog, *p1, k1; repeat from * to last 3 stitches, p1, k2tog. (19 stitches)
Row 7: P1, *p1, k1; repeat from * to last 2 stitches, p2.
Row 8: *K1, p1; repeat from * to last stitch, k1.
Row 9: P1, *p1, k1; repeat from * to last 2 stitches, p2.

Repeat rows 2-9 until 7 stitches remain.

Row 10: K2tog, k1, p1, k1, k2tog. (5 stitches)
Row 11: P1, k1, p1, k1, p1.
Row 12: K2tog, p1, k2tog. (3 stitches)
Row 13: P3.
Row 14: K3tog.

Break yarn and pull through remaining stitch.

Weave in ends.

ALL TRIANGLES

FINISHING
Block all the triangles to 16cm/6½" wide and 15cm/6" tall. You might find it easier to cut a template from some cardboard. Lightly dampen the triangles and pin them out to the right size.

We blocked our bunting using a steam iron on medium heat (test your iron on a scrap of yarn to check it comes out OK. Wool can be ironed directly but if you choose to substitute a synthetic yarn or blend you need to be careful to avoid melting the yarn). You can pin directly to the ironing board and gently press into shape – this is the best way to ensure that the ribbed and welted triangles are the same shape as the others.

marina poncho

Made from just two rectangles in garter stitch, this poncho couldn't be easier to knit.

YARN
baa ram ewe Dovestone Natural Chunky
C1: shade 1, 360m/393 yds (3 balls)
C2: shade 2, 360m/393 yds (3 balls)

NEEDLES
6.5mm (US 10.5) straight needles

GAUGE
14 stitches x 24 rows = 10cm/4" in garter stitch, after blocking
Getting the right gauge on this project is quite important, and you may need to change needle size to obtain the right gauge. If your gauge is not correct you might run out of yarn and the neck hole on your poncho might be too small. As long as your finished pieces are close to the right size after blocking your project will be fine.

ABBREVIATIONS
A list of standard abbreviations appears on the inside back cover.

FINISHED SIZE
79cm/31" from neck to bottom point at front or back.

Note: the measurements given for knitting are based on how much Dovestone Natural Chunky will stretch after blocking. If you use a different yarn it may not stretch as much. If this is the case, you will need to knit your pieces longer to start with.

PONCHO

PIECE A
Cast on 77 sts using C1.
Knit every row until piece measures 66cm (26"). Cast off.

PIECE B
Cast on 77 sts using C2.

Knit every row until piece measures 66cm (26"). Cast off.

FINISHING
Block the pieces as follows: wash and squeeze out the excess water from the pieces as described on page 17.
Lay each piece flat to dry so that it measures 56cm (22") wide and 84cm (33") long.

TO SEW UP
Sew the cast on edge of piece A to one long edge of piece B so that they form an 'L' shape.

Then sew the short edge of B to the long edge of A. Use the diagrams and photos to help see which piece should be sewn to what.

SCHEMATIC

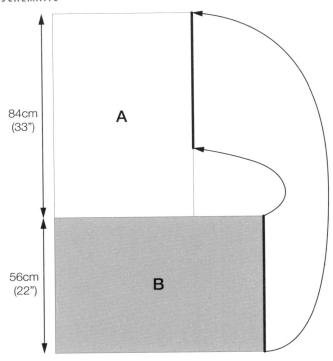

84cm (33")

A

56cm (22")

B

nelly cardigan

An oversized cardigan knitted in squishy garter stitch for maximum cosiness.

CHUNKY CARDIGAN

YARN
Dovestone Natural Chunky
Shade 4, 1620m/1772yds [14 balls]

NEEDLES
6.5mm (US 10.5) straight needles

GAUGE
14 stitches x 24 rows = 10cm/4" in garter stitch after blocking

FINISHED SIZE
139.5cm (55") finished bust measurement with 17cm (6¾")
overlap at front
The cardigan shown is modelled with approx 51cm (20") of
ease (see notes on fit)

ARAN CARDIGAN (NOT SHOWN)

YARN
Dovestone Natural Aran, 1910m/2089yds (12 skeins)

NEEDLES
5mm (US 8) straight needles

GAUGE
18 stitches x 34 rows = 10cm/4" in garter stitch after blocking

FINISHED SIZE
108.5cm (42½") finished bust measurement with 13.5cm
(5¼") overlap at front

FIT
This sweater is intended to be worn oversized with plenty of
ease. At baa ram ewe HQ everyone could wear the chunky
cardigan shown, on bust sizes ranging from 81.5-127cm
(32"-50"). If you are petite or prefer a slightly less oversized
look you could choose the aran version, which has shorter
and narrower sleeves as well as being smaller in the bust.
The instructions for the back and fronts are the same for
the Chunky and Aran cardigans, but there are different
instructions for the sleeves. Please make sure you knit the
right sleeves for your yarn!

GAUGE
Because the sweater is meant to be oversized, exact gauge
is not essential. However, if your gauge is different than listed,
you may use more yarn than specified and your sweater
will come out a different size. A small difference in gauge in
a large item like a sweater can have a big effect upon the
finished size. You may need to change needle size to obtain
the right gauge.

ABBREVIATIONS
A list of standard abbreviations appears on the inside back
cover.

BOTH CARDIGANS

BACK
Cast on 96 stitches.
Knit every row until piece measures 71cm (28") from cast on edge.
Cast off.

FRONTS (MAKE 2)
Cast on 60 stitches.

Knit every row until piece measures 71cm (28") from cast on edge.
Cast off.

CHUNKY CARDIGAN

SLEEVES (MAKE 2)

Cast on 70 stitches.

Rows 1-4: Knit.
Row 5: K1, k2tog, knit to end. (There will now be 69 stitches)
Row 6: K1, k2tog, knit to end. (68 stitches)
Rows 7-10: Knit.
Repeat rows 5-10 until 50 stitches remain.

Row 11: K1, k2tog, knit to end. (49 stitches)
Row 12: K1, k2tog, knit to end. (48 stitches)
Rows 13-14: Knit.
Repeat rows 11-14 until 36 stitches remain.

Knit every row until piece measures 44.5cm (17½") from cast on edge.

Cast off.

ARAN CARDIGAN

SLEEVES (MAKE 2)
Cast on 76 stitches.

Rows 1-4: Knit.
Row 5: K1, k2tog, knit to end. (There will now be 75 stitches)
Row 6: K1, k2tog, knit to end. (74 stitches)
Rows 7-10: Knit.
Repeat rows 5-10 until 36 stitches remain.

Knit every row until piece measures 41cm (16") from cast on edge.
Cast off.

CHUNKY CARDIGAN

FINISHING
Block all pieces and weave in ends.

TO MAKE UP
Sew each front to the back for 27.5cm (10¾") along shoulder seam.
Fold sleeve in half lengthways and mark midpoint of cast on edge.
Line up midpoint with shoulder seam and sew sleeve to back and front.
Repeat for other sleeve.
Sew side seams and sleeve seams.

ARAN CARDIGAN

FINISHING
Block all pieces and weave in ends.

TO MAKE UP
Sew each front to the back for 19.5cm (7¾") along shoulder seam.
Fold sleeve in half lengthways and mark midpoint of cast on edge.
Line up midpoint with shoulder seam and sew sleeve to back and front.
Repeat for other sleeve.
Sew side seams and sleeve seams.

MEASUREMENTS

	Bust/chest	Overlap at front	Length (neck to hem)	Upper arm circumference	Neck width	Sleeve length (underarm to cuff)
Chunky (cm)	139.5	17	71	51	15	44.5
Chunky (in)	55	6¾	28	20	6	17½
Aran (cm)	108.5	13.5	71	43	15	41
Aran (in)	42½	5¼	28	17	6	16

SCHEMATIC

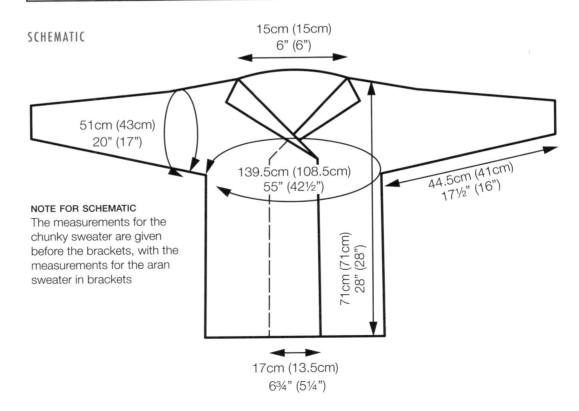

NOTE FOR SCHEMATIC
The measurements for the chunky sweater are given before the brackets, with the measurements for the aran sweater in brackets

15cm (15cm)
6" (6")

51cm (43cm)
20" (17")

139.5cm (108.5cm)
55" (42½")

44.5cm (41cm)
17½" (16")

71cm (71cm)
28" (28")

17cm (13.5cm)
6¾" (5¼")

baa ram ewe LEARN TO KNIT AT HOME   31

baa ram ewe LEARN TO KNIT AT HOME

howard blanket

This blanket is made in 5 strips which are sewn together. It's made completely in garter stitch and each piece is only 20cm wide, which makes it easy to knit on straight needles.

The length for each colour has been specified in ridges. When you knit garter stitch, it forms ridges that are easy to count – much easier than counting individual rows. Every ridge is two rows. Make sure you count on the right side of the work – I suggest you mark the right side with a safety pin on the first row so you can tell which is which.

YARN
Dovestone Natural Chunky
C1: shade 1, 240m/263yds [2 balls]
C2: shade 2, 240m/263yds [2 balls]
C3: shade 3, 240m/263yds [2 balls]
C4: shade 4, 240m/263yds [2 balls]
C5: shade 5, 240m/263yds [2 balls]

NEEDLES
6.5mm (US 10.5) straight needles

GAUGE
14 stitches x 24 rows = 10cm/4" in garter stitch (knit every row), after blocking
Getting the right gauge for this project is fairly important. If you knit at the wrong gauge you might run out of yarn, or end up with a very small blanket. You may need to change needle size to obtain the right gauge.

ABBREVIATIONS
A list of standard abbreviations appears on the inside back cover.

FINISHED SIZE
100cm x 125cm (39½" x 49¼")

STRIP A
Using C1, cast on 28 sts.
Work in garter stitch (knit every row) for 23 ridges (46 rows), finishing after a WS row. Break yarn.

Using C2, work in garter stitch until you have worked 38 ridges in this colour, finishing after a WS row. Break yarn.

Using C3, work in garter stitch until you have worked 37 ridges in this colour, finishing after a WS row. Break yarn.

Using C4, work in garter stitch until you have worked 22 ridges in this colour, finishing after a WS row. Break yarn.

Using C5, work in garter stitch until you have worked 30 ridges in this colour, finishing after a WS row. Cast off.

STRIP B
Using C1, cast on 28 sts.
Work in garter stitch for 30 ridges, finishing after a WS row. Break yarn.

Using C2, work in garter stitch until you have worked 15 ridges in this colour, finishing after a WS row. Break yarn.

Using C3, work in garter stitch until you have worked 30 ridges in this colour, finishing after a WS row. Break yarn.

Using C4, work in garter stitch until you have worked 38 ridges in this colour, finishing after a WS row. Break yarn.

Using C5, work in garter stitch until you have worked 37 ridges in this colour, finishing after a WS row. Cast off.

STRIP C
Using C1, cast on 28 sts.
Work in garter stitch for 37 ridges, finishing after a WS row. Break yarn.

Using C2, work in garter stitch until you have worked 30 ridges in this colour, finishing after a WS row. Break yarn.

Using C3, work in garter stitch until you have worked 30 ridges in this colour, finishing after a WS row. Break yarn.

Using C4, work in garter stitch until you have worked 30 ridges in this colour, finishing after a WS row. Break yarn.

Using C5, work in garter stitch until you have worked 23 ridges in this colour, finishing after a WS row. Cast off.

STRIP D

Using C1, cast on 28 sts.
Work in garter stitch for 22 ridges, finishing after a WS row. Break yarn.

Using C2, work in garter stitch until you have worked 37 ridges in this colour, finishing after a WS row. Break yarn.

Using C3, work in garter stitch until you have worked 23 ridges in this colour, finishing after a WS row. Break yarn.

Using C4, work in garter stitch until you have worked 23 ridges in this colour, finishing after a WS row. Break yarn.

Using C5, work in garter stitch until you have worked 45 ridges in this colour, finishing after a WS row. Cast off.

STRIP E

Using C1, cast on 28 sts.
Work in garter stitch for 38 ridges, finishing after a WS row. Break yarn.

Using C2, work in garter stitch until you have worked 30 ridges in this colour, finishing after a WS row. Break yarn.

Using C3, work in garter stitch until you have worked 30 ridges in this colour, finishing after a WS row. Break yarn.

Using C4, work in garter stitch until you have worked 37 ridges in this colour, finishing after a WS row. Break yarn.

Using C5, work in garter stitch until you have worked 15 ridges in this colour, finishing after a WS row. Cast off.

FINISHING

Block all the strips (see blocking instructions on page 17).

Sew the strips together in order from A to E using the diagram and photos for reference. For the best results you can use shade 1 to sew up at the light end, swapping to shade 3 to sew up the middle and shade 5 to sew up the dark end. If you want to sew with just one colour then I suggest using shade 3.

SCHEMATIC

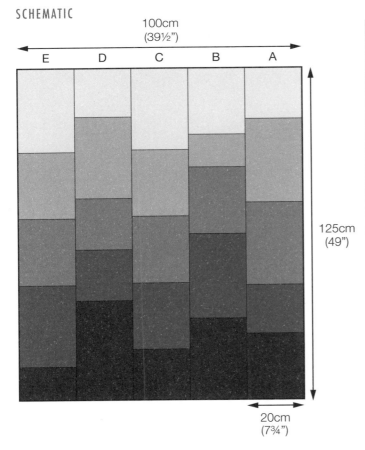

100cm
(39½")

E   D   C   B   A

125cm
(49")

20cm
(7¾")

walter blanket and cushions

Bold chevrons make a perfect statement piece for your bed or sofa. The zig-zag pattern is created using increases and decreases, with stitch markers to help you keep everything in the right place.

ARAN BLANKET

YARN
baa ram ewe Dovestone Natural Aran
C1: Shade 5, 510m/558 yds [3 skeins]
C2: Shade 7, 510m/558 yds [3 skeins]
C3: Shade 1, 510m/558 yds [3 skeins]

NEEDLES AND NOTIONS
5mm (US 8) circular needle, 100cm (40") or longer
Stitch markers

GAUGE
18 stitches x 34 rows = 10cm/4" in garter stitch, after blocking

FINISHED SIZE
122cm x 101.5cm (48" x 40")

ABBREVIATIONS
A list of standard abbreviations appears on the inside back cover.

CHUNKY BLANKET

YARN
baa ram ewe Dovestone Natural Chunky
C1: Shade 5, 660m/722 yds [6 balls]
C2: Shade 3, 660m/722 yds [6 balls]
C3: Shade 1, 660m/722 yds [6 balls]

NEEDLES
6.5mm (US 10.5) circular needle, 100cm (40") or longer

GAUGE
14 stitches x 24 rows = 10cm/4" in garter stitch, after blocking

FINISHED SIZE
159cm x 127cm (62½" x 50")

Getting the right gauge is not critical for this project as your blanket will still work well even if it comes out a different size! However, if your gauge is very different you may run out of yarn. You may need to change needle size to obtain the right gauge.

ARAN CUSHION

YARN

baa ram ewe Dovestone Natural Aran
C1: Shade 5, 300m/328yds [2 skeins]
C2: Shade 7, 300m/328yds [2 skeins]
C3: Shade 1, 300m/328yds [2 skeins]

NEEDLES AND NOTIONS

5mm (US 8) circular needle, 60cm (24") or longer
1 large button, about 5cm/2" diameter.
1 cushion pad, 48cm x 48cm (19" x 19")

GAUGE

18 stitches x 34 rows = 10cm/4" in garter stitch, after blocking

FINISHED SIZE

49cm x 49cm (19½" x 19½")

CHUNKY CUSHION

YARN

baa ram ewe Dovestone Natural Chunky
C1: Shade 5, 360m/394 yds [3 balls]
C2: Shade 3, 360m/394 yds [3 balls]
C3: Shade 1, 360m/394 yds [3 balls]

NEEDLES AND NOTIONS

6.5mm (US 10.5) circular needle, 60cm (24") or longer
1 large button, about 5cm/2" diameter.
1 cushion pad, 63.5cm x 63.5cm (25" x 25")

GAUGE

14 stitches x 24 rows = 10cm/4" in garter stitch, after blocking

FINISHED SIZE

63.5cm x 63.5cm (25" x 25")

BOTH BLANKETS

Using C1, [cast on 30 stitches, place marker] 9 times, cast on 30 sts. 300 stitches in total have been cast on.

Row 1 (RS): [K1, kfb, knit to 2 stitches before marker, k2tog, slip marker, k2tog, knit to 2 stitches before marker, kfb, k1] 5 times.
Row 2 (WS): Knit.

These two rows form the chevron pattern. Repeat these two rows 11 more times. Break yarn.

Join C2 and work these two rows 12 times. Break yarn.

Join C3 and work these two rows 12 times. Break yarn. Continuing to work in pattern, work six more stripes in this order: C1, C2, C3, C1, C2 and C3.

Cast off using C3.
Weave in ends and block using instructions on page 17.

BOTH CUSHIONS

Using C1 [cast on 30 stitches, place marker] 3 times, cast on 30 stitches. 120 stitches in total have been cast on.

Row 1 (RS): [K1, kfb, knit to 2 stitches before marker, k2tog, slip marker, k2tog, knit to 2 stitches before marker, kfb, k1, slip marker] twice.
Row 2 (WS): Knit.

These two rows form the chevron pattern. Repeat these two rows 11 more times. Break yarn.

Join C2 and work these two rows 12 times. Break yarn.

Join C3 and work these two rows 12 times. Break yarn.

Continuing to work in chevron pattern, work stripes in sequence C1, C2, C3 until piece measures 110cm (43½") for an aran cushion or 140cm (55") for a chunky cushion, measured along the edge of the piece. When you have reached the required length, complete the stripe.

Cast off.

FINISHING

Block piece. Lay the cushion piece flat as shown in the diagram with the wrong side facing. The chevron design means that the ends are different from each other so make sure you match the diagram.

Measure 30cm (12") for the aran cushion or 38cm (15") for the chunky cushion from the left hand end along the edge and fold the left side over at this point. Sew up the cushion sides on both edges.

Now overlap the other end of the cushion so that the cushion measures 49cm (19½") along the edge for the aran cushion or 63.5cm (25"). Sew up the cushion sides on both edges.

Sew the button on the central point on the top part of the overlap. Make a button loop (see page 11) in the centre of the 'valley' below the button (see photos for reference).

Insert the cushion pad and fasten the button.

SCHEMATIC

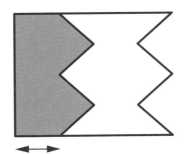

30cm (12") ARAN

38cm (15") CHUNKY

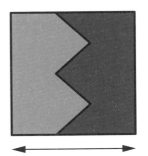

49cm (19½") ARAN

63.5cm (25") CHUNKY

clem sweater

A unisex, oversized boxy sweater with a boat neck. Warm, cosy and perfect for curling up on the sofa.

CHUNKY SWEATER

YARN
Dovestone Natural Chunky
Shade 2, 1555m/1700yds [9 balls]

NEEDLES
6.5mm (US 10.5) straight needles

GAUGE
14 stitches x 20 rows to 10cm/4" in stocking stitch, after blocking
14 stitches x 24 rows to 10cm/4" in garter stitch, after blocking

ABBREVIATIONS
A list of standard abbreviations appears on the inside back cover.

FINISHED SIZE
139.5cm (55") finished bust measurement
The sweater shown is modelled with approx 51cm (20") of ease (see notes on fit)

ARAN SWEATER (NOT SHOWN)

YARN
Dovestone Natural Aran, 1310m/1433yds (8 skeins)

NEEDLES
5mm (US 8) straight

GAUGE
18 stitches x 26 rows = 10cm/4" in stocking stitch, after blocking
18 stitches x 34 rows = 10cm/4" in garter stitch, after blocking

FINISHED SIZE
108.5cm (42½") finished bust/chest measurement

FIT
This sweater is intended to be worn oversized with plenty of ease. At baa ram ewe HQ everyone could wear the chunky sweater shown, on bust sizes ranging from 81.5-127cm (32"-50"). If you are petite or prefer a slightly less oversized look you could choose the aran version, which has shorter and narrower sleeves as well as being smaller in the bust.

GAUGE
Because the sweater is meant to be oversized, exact gauge is not essential. However, if your gauge is different you may use more yarn than specified and your sweater will come out a different size. A small difference in gauge in a large item like a sweater can have a fairly big effect upon the finished size. You may need to change needle size to obtain the right gauge.

BOTH SWEATERS
BACK AND FRONT (MAKE 2)
Cast on 96 stitches.
Knit every row until piece measures 4cm (1½") from cast on edge.

Work body of sweater as follows:
Row 1 (RS): Knit.
Row 2 (WS): Purl.
Repeat rows 1 and 2 until piece measures 33cm (13") from the cast on edge, ending after a purl row.
Knit every row until piece measures 71cm (28") from the cast on edge.
Cast off.

CHUNKY SWEATER
SLEEVES (MAKE 2)
Cast on 70 stitches.
Row 1 (RS): Knit.
Row 2 (WS): Purl.
Repeat rows 1-2 two more times.

Row 3: K1, k2tog, knit to last 3 stitches, k2tog, k1. (There will now be 68 stitches)
Row 4: Purl
Row 5: Knit.
Row 6: Purl.
Repeat rows 3-6 until 36 stitches remain.

Repeat rows 5 and 6 until piece measures 42cm (16½") from the cast on edge, ending after a purl row.
Knit every row until piece measures 44.5cm (17½") from the cast on edge.
Cast off.

ARAN SWEATER
SLEEVES (MAKE 2)
Cast on 76 stitches.
Row 1 (RS): Knit.
Row 2 (WS): Purl.
Repeat rows 1-2 four more times.

Row 3: K1, k2tog, knit to last 3 stitches, k2tog, k1. (There will now be 74 stitches)
Row 4: Purl
Row 5: Knit.
Row 6: Purl.
Repeat rows 3-6 until 40 stitches remain.

Repeat rows 5 and 6 until piece measures 37cm (14½") from cast on edge, ending after a purl row.
Knit every row until piece measures 41cm (16") from the cast on edge.
Cast off.

CHUNKY SWEATER
FINISHING
Block all pieces and weave in ends.

Remember when sewing up that the short garter stitch section on the front and back pieces is at the top of the sweater and the deep garter stitch section is at the bottom. Use the photos for reference.

Sew front to the back for 21.5cm (8½") along each shoulder seam, leaving a gap of 26.5cm (10½") in the centre for the neck.

You can adjust the width of the neck hole to make it smaller if you like, but make sure you don't sew it up so small that you can't get your head through the neck hole!

Fold sleeve in half lengthways and mark the midpoint of cast on edge.
Line up midpoint with shoulder seam and sew sleeve to back and front.
Repeat for other sleeve.
Sew sleeve seams and side seams, leaving bottom 4cm (1½") of side seams not sewn if desired.

ARAN SWEATER
FINISHING
Block all pieces and weave in ends.

Remember when sewing up that the short garter stitch section on the front and back pieces is at the top of the sweater and the deep garter stitch section is at the bottom. Use the photos for reference.

Sew front to the back for 14cm (5½") along each shoulder seam, leaving a gap of 25.5cm (10") in the centre for the neck.

You can adjust the width of the neck hole to make it smaller if you like, but make sure you don't sew it up so small that you can't get your head through the neck hole!

Fold sleeve in half lengthways and mark midpoint of cast on edge.
Line up midpoint with shoulder seam and sew sleeve to back and front.
Repeat for other sleeve.
Sew sleeve seams and side seams, leaving bottom 4cm (1½") of side seams not sewn if desired.

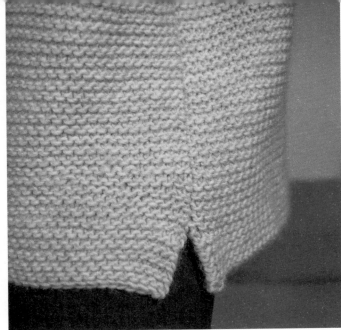

MEASUREMENTS

	Bust/chest	Length (neck to hem)	Upper arm circumference	Neck width	Sleeve length (underarm to cuff)
Chunky (cm)	139.5	71	51	26.5	44.5
Chunky (in)	55	28	20	10½	17½
Aran (cm)	108.5	71	43	25.5	41
Aran (in)	42½	28	17	10	16

SCHEMATIC

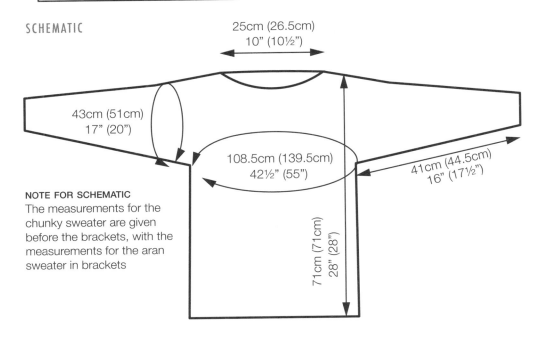

25cm (26.5cm)
10" (10½")

43cm (51cm)
17" (20")

108.5cm (139.5cm)
42½" (55")

41cm (44.5cm)
16" (17½")

71cm (71cm)
28" (28")

NOTE FOR SCHEMATIC
The measurements for the chunky sweater are given before the brackets, with the measurements for the aran sweater in brackets

baa ram ewe LEARN TO KNIT AT HOME

marley the owl cushion

Although Marley is made of quite a few parts, he's easy to knit and cute as a button (or two!)

YARN

baa ram ewe Dovestone Natural Aran
MC: Shade 8, 286m/313yds [2 skeins]
CC: Shade 6, 140m/153yds [1 skein]

NEEDLES AND NOTIONS

5mm (US 8) straight needles
Two large (5cm/2") buttons for eyes **or** felt to make sewn eyes
30cm x 40cm (12" x 16") cushion pad

GAUGE

18 stitches x 36 rows = 10cm/4" in garter stitch, after blocking
18 stitches x 26 rows = 10cm/4" in stocking stitch, after blocking
Getting the right gauge is fairly important for this project and you may need to change needle size to obtain the right gauge. If you knit too loosely, you might be able to see the cushion pad through the stitches and Marley's wings could be a bit floppy!

ABBREVIATIONS

A list of standard abbreviations appears on the inside back cover.

FINISHED SIZE

30cm x 40cm (12" x 16") when sewn up (excluding feet and tassels).

BODY AND HEAD

Cast on 56 stitches using MC and 5mm needles.
Knit every row until work measures 34cm (13½") from cast on edge. Break yarn.
Change to CC.
Row 1 (RS): Knit.
Row 2 (WS): Purl.
Repeat rows 1 and 2 until work measures 80cm (31½") from cast on edge, ending after a purl row. Break yarn.

Change to MC.
Knit every row until work measures 96cm (38") from cast on edge.
Cast off.

Weave in ends and block.

SEW UP BODY AND HEAD

With right side facing, fold the cast on edge down 17cm (6¾") so that it lines up with the first colour change. This forms the head. Referring to page 12 for instructions, sew the sides of the cushion down using MC and mattress stitch for garter. Flip the top part of the cushion inside out.

Fold the bottom part of the cushion up, lining up the colour change so that the contrast colour section is folded in half. There will be a section of MC that overlaps – this will ensure there is no gap at the back of the cushion. Sew up the sides of the cushion, using CC and mattress stitch for stocking stitch on the CC section and MC and mattress stitch for garter on the MC section.

Flip the top part of the cushion right side out.

FEET (MAKE 2)

(optional – his feet are the trickiest part – give them a go, but if you are stumped, he will manage fine without them!)
Cast on 9 sts using MC.
Row 1: Knit.
Row 2: K1, kfb, k to end. (There will now be 10 stitches)
Repeat row 2 five more times. (15 stitches)
Row 3: Knit.

The toes are now worked separately over groups of 5 stitches at a time as follows:
Row 4: K2tog, K3, turn work. You will now work on these 4 stitches only.
Row 5: K2tog, k2.
Row 6: K2tog, k1.
Row 7: K2tog.
Cut yarn and pull through remaining stitch.

Rejoin yarn to remaining 10 stitches.
Repeat rows 4-7 to make the next toe.
Cut yarn and pull through remaining stitch.

Rejoin yarn to remaining 5 stitches.
Repeat rows 4-7 to make one more toe.
Cut yarn and pull through remaining stitch.

Weave in ends and block.

WINGS (MAKE 2)

Cast on 1 stitch using MC. (To cast on just one stitch, make a slip knot and put it on your needle.)
Row 1: Kfb. (There will now be 2 stitches)
Row 2: Kfb, k1. (3 stitches)
Rows 3-4: Knit.
Row 5: Kfb, k2. (4 stitches)
Row 6: K1, kfb, k2. (5 stitches)
Rows 7-8: Knit.
Row 9: K1, kfb, k3. (6 stitches)
Row 10: K1, kfb, k4. (7 stitches)
Rows 11-12: Knit.
Row 13: K1, kfb, k to end. (8 stitches)
Row 14: K1, kfb, k to end. (9 stitches)
Repeat rows 11-14 until there are 33 stitches.
Knit 2 rows.
Cast off.

Weave in ends and block.

BEAK

Cast on 15 stitches using CC.
Row 1 (RS): Knit.
Row 2 (WS): Purl.
Row 3: K1, k2tog, k2, k2tog, k1, k2tog, k2, k2tog, k1. (11 stitches)
Row 4: Purl.
Row 5: K1, k2tog, k2tog, k1, k2tog, k2tog, k1. (7 stitches)
Row 6: Purl.
Row 7: K1, k2tog, k1, k2tog, k1. (5 stitches)
Break yarn, leaving a tail of approximately 30cm (12") for sewing up. Thread the tail of yarn through the remaining live stitches using a sewing up needle. This will gather the stitches together to make the point of the beak.

Fold in half and whipstitch along the edge of the beak. The rest of the tail can be left to attach the beak to the head.

TASSELS (MAKE 2)

Using CC, wrap yarn about 7 times around a card about 10cm/4" wide. Cut yarn on one end, tie another piece of yarn around the middle of the bunch and knot to secure. Cut one more piece of yarn and wrap it around the top of the bunch to form the tassel.

TO FINISH THE OWL

Sew the wings to the bottom of the head at the colour change, lining up the point of the wing with the side seam.

Sew the feet to the bottom of the cushion, spaced about 5cm (2") apart.

Sew buttons to the head, using photos as a guide.

Alternatively, if you prefer, or if the cushion is to be given to a child, cut circles of felt with 5cm (2") diameter and sew on for eyes. I suggest using blanket stitch and yarn for a cute, rustic effect, but you could whipstitch around the edges or use matching sewing thread for an invisible effect. Finish with a cross in the centre of each eye in dark coloured yarn to define the eye.

Sew beak to head using photos as a guide.

Sew a tassel to each top corner, and insert cushion pad.

edie armwarmers

These armwarmers are a great project to practice ribbing. They're very easy to knit as they are made as a flat rectangle with no increases or decreases. Perfect for snuggling up with a mug of tea and a good book!

YARN
Dovestone Natural Chunky
Shade 3, 110m/120 yds [1 ball]

NEEDLES
5.5mm (US 9) straight needles.

GAUGE
24 sts x 22 rows =10cm/4" in 2x2 rib, unstretched, after blocking.

Getting the right gauge is fairly important for this pattern. If you knit too loosely you will run out of yarn and your armwarmers might be baggy. If you knit too tightly your armwarmers might be too small to fit on your arms. You may need to change needle size to obtain the right gauge.

ABBREVIATIONS
A list of standard abbreviations appears on the inside back cover.

FINISHED SIZE
Length: 28cm (11")
Circumference: 16cm (6¼") unstretched

ARMWARMERS (MAKE 2)
Cast on 38 sts. It is important that the cast on is not too tight as otherwise your armwarmer might be too tight to go over your arm. If you find you do cast on too tightly, try using needles at least 2 sizes bigger for the cast on row.

Row 1 (RS): K2, *p2, k2; repeat from * to end of row.
Row 2 (WS): P2, *k2, p2;repeat from * to end of row.

Repeat rows 1 and 2 until the piece measures 28cm (11") from cast on edge.

Cast off.

Weave in ends and block pieces following instructions on page 17.

SEWING UP
Fold piece in half lengthways. Check your cast on and cast off edges and choose the stretchiest to be the end closest to your elbow. Sew up from the bottom edge for 17cm (6¾") and fasten off. Leave a gap of 6cm (2½") for the thumbhole, and sew up the remaining 5cm (2") at the top of the mitt.

baa ram ewe LEARN TO KNIT AT HOME

nora socks

These socks are made as a simple ribbed tube, ideal for a cosy sock to wear around the house or in bed. They're knitted flat in one piece and sewn up along the toe and up one side.

YARN
Dovestone Natural Aran, 240m/263 yds [2 skeins]
Shown in Shade 6

NEEDLES AND NOTIONS
4mm (US 6) straight needles
1 stitch marker

GAUGE
38 stitches x 30 rows = 10cm/4" in 2x2 rib, unstretched, after blocking
(approx 22 stitches to 10cm/4" when lightly stretched and 17 stitches to 10cm/4" when fully stretched)
22 stitches x 30 rows = 10cm/4" in stocking stitch

Getting the right gauge is important for this pattern and you may need to change needle size to obtain the right gauge. The socks are knitted on smaller needles than usual so that the rib is stretchy – this is important for the socks to fit well. If you knit too loosely your socks will be baggy and could slide off your feet. If you knit too tightly the socks might not fit your feet!

ABBREVIATIONS
A list of standard abbreviations appears on the back cover.

FINISHED SIZE
Circumference: approx 13cm (5"), unstretched
One size fits most feet from approx UK size 1 (US 3/EU 33) upwards.

TIP
Using a marker on the toe makes it easier to get the decreases in the right place. The marker is placed on the needle between two stitches. When you come to the instruction to slip marker you simply use the tip of the right needle to pick up the marker and move it from the left needle to the right needle.

SOCKS (MAKE 2)
Cast on 50 stitches. Make sure you don't cast on too tightly as this could make your sock difficult to put on. If you find your cast on is tight, try casting on using needles at least two sizes bigger and then swap to the correct size to begin knitting.

Row 1 (RS): *K2, p2; repeat from * to last 2 stitches, k2.
Row 2 (WS): *P2, k2; repeat from * to last 2 stitches, p2.

Repeat these two rows until the sock measures 43.5cm (17"), ending after row 2. You can make your socks longer if you like, but make sure you allow 5 g of yarn after knitting the ribbed section for each sock to knit the toe and sew up.

SHAPE TOE
Row 1 (RS): K25, place marker, knit to end.
Row 2 (WS): Purl.
Row 3: K1, k2tog, knit to 3 stitches before marker, k2tog, k1, slip marker, k1, k2tog, knit to 3 stitches before end, k2tog, k1. (There will now be 46 stitches)
Row 4: Purl.

Repeat rows 3 and 4 two more times. (38 stitches)

Cast off. Remove the marker when you come to it.

Weave in ends and block (see blocking instructions on page 12).

Fold in half and sew across the toe and up the side of the sock. I recommend using mattress stitch to sew the side seam.

pearl blanket and cushion

These cosy knits are super thick and cuddly because the yarn is held double and worked on a larger needle (this also means they are quicker to knit). The blankets and cushion are worked in a bold 6x6 rib pattern.

YARN

baa ram ewe Dovestone Natural Chunky, Shade 1 (held double throughout)
Small (large) blanket: 960 (2400)m/1048 (2620) yds [8 (20) balls]
Small (large) bed runner: 1200 (1800)m/1310(1965) yds [10 (15) balls]
Cushion: 720m/786yds [6 balls]

NEEDLES AND NOTIONS

Blanket: 10mm (US 15) circular needles, length will depend on size of blanket – 100cm (40") is recommended for the small size
Cushions: 10mm (US 15) straight needles
48cm x 48cm (19" x 19") cushion pad (for cushion only)

ABBREVIATIONS

A list of standard abbreviations appears on the inside back cover.

GAUGE

10 stitches x 15 rows = 10cm/4" in 6x6 rib pattern with yarn held double
10 stitches x 15 rows = 10cm/4" in stocking stitch with yarn held double, after blocking
Getting the correct gauge is fairly important for this project and you may need to change needle size to obtain the right gauge. If your gauge is different you might run out of yarn and your finished item might not come out at the specified size. In particular, the back of the cushion needs the right amount of overlap to completely cover the cushion pad inside, so the cover should be two and a half times as long as it is wide.

SIZES

Small blanket: approximately 96.5cm x 86cm (38" x 34")
Large blanket: approx 134cm x 134cm (53" x 53")
Small bed runner: approx 134cm x 68.5cm (53" x 27")
Large bed runner: approx 206.5cm x 68.5cm (81" x 27")
Cushion: 48cm x 48cm (19" x 19"), size of knitted piece 48cm x 120cm (19" x 47½")

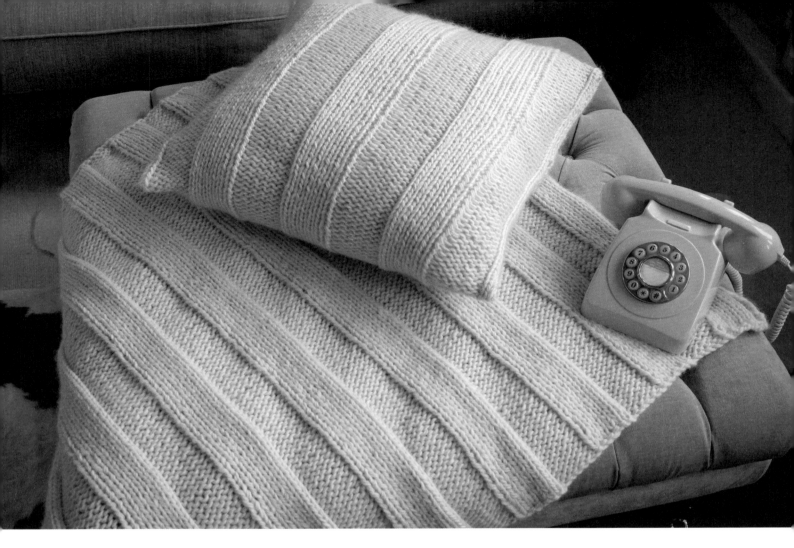

BLANKETS AND BED RUNNERS

Using yarn held double cast on as follows:
For a small blanket: cast on 96 stitches.
For a large blanket or small bed runner: cast on 132 stitches.
For a large bed runner: cast on 204 stitches.

Row 1 (RS): K3, *p6, k6; repeat from * to last 9 stitches, p6, k3.
Row 2 (WS): P3, *k6, p6; repeat from * to last 9 stitches, k6, p3.
Repeat rows 1 and 2 until you reach the required length. It doesn't matter whether you finish after a RS or WS row. Make sure that you allow sufficient yarn to cast off (at least 5 times the finished width of the piece).

Cast off in pattern.
Weave in the ends and block.

CUSHION

Using yarn held double, cast on 48 stitches.

Row 1 (RS): K3, *p6, k6; repeat from * to last 9 stitches, p6, k3.
Row 2 (WS): P3, *k6, p6; repeat from * to last 9 stitches, k6, p3.
Repeat rows 1 and 2 until the piece measures 120cm (47½") from the cast on edge. It doesn't matter whether you finish after a RS or WS row. Cast off in pattern.

Weave in ends and block.
Use a single strand of yarn for sewing up.

To sew up, fold up the bottom edge of the cushion 36cm (14¼") and sew the side seam on each side using mattress stitch. Flip this section inside out. Fold up the other edge of the cushion 36cm (14¼") and sew side seams – there will be an overlap at the back of the cushion. Flip the cushion the right way out and insert cushion pad.

norman and sybil hot water bottle cosies

Sleepy Sybil and simple Norman are ready to warm up your bed for a cosy, restful night. Just make a sheep head and legs to turn your plain Norman hot water bottle cosy into a cute Sybil!

NORMAN HOT WATER BOTTLE COSY

YARN
baa ram ewe Dovestone Natural Aran
160 (205)m/175 (224)yds [1 (2) skeins]
Shown in Shade 3 in size small.

NEEDLES
4mm (US 6) straight needles

GAUGE
38 stitches x 30 rows = 10cm/4" in 2x2 rib, unstretched, after blocking
Approximately 22 stitches to 10cm/4" when lightly stretched and 17 stitches to 10cm/4" when fully stretched.
22 stitches x 30 rows = 10cm/4" in stocking stitch, after blocking

Getting the right gauge is important for this pattern. If you knit too loosely or tightly your hot water bottle cover might not come out the size specified in the pattern, and might not fit your hot water bottle. You may need to change needle size to obtain the right gauge.

ABBREVIATIONS
A list of standard abbreviations appears on the inside back cover.

FINISHED SIZE
Small (large), to fit a hot water bottle approx 31cm (12¼")
from top of neck to bottom and 35-40cm (40-45cm) /
13¾-15¾" (15¾-17¾") circumference around middle.
Size small has a plain neck and size large is long enough to turn over at the neck.

SYBIL THE SHEEP HOT WATER BOTTLE COSY

YARN AND NOTIONS
baa ram ewe Dovestone Natural Aran in Shade 4, 100m/109 yds [1 skein]
1 Norman hot water bottle cosy (shown in size large using Shade 1)
Toy stuffing
A small amount of light coloured yarn for embroidery
Tapestry needle

NORMAN HOT WATER BOTTLE COSY

MULTI SIZE PATTERN

This pattern is written for small and large sizes, written as small (large). If you are making the small size, use the stitch counts and measurements before the brackets. If you are making the large size, use the stitch counts and measurements in brackets.

Cast on 38 (46) stitches.

Row 1 (RS): *K2, p2; repeat from * to last 2 stitches, k2.
Row 2 (WS): *P2, k2; repeat from * to last 2 stitches, p2.

Repeat rows 1 and 2 until piece measures 71 (84) cm/ 28" (33") from the cast on edge.

Cast off in pattern.

Block, using instructions on page 17.

Fold piece in half with wrong sides together. Sew up each side of the cosy using mattress stitch.

Weave in ends.

SYBIL'S HEAD

Cast on 16 stitches.

Row 1 (RS): Knit.
Row 2 (WS): Purl.
Repeat rows 1 and 2 once more.

Row 3: K1, kfb, knit to last 2 stitches, kfb, k1. (There will now be 18 stitches)
Row 4: Purl.
Row 5: Knit.
Row 6: Purl.
Row 7: Knit.
Row 8: Purl.
Repeat rows 3 to 8 twice more. (22 stitches)

Row 9: K1, k2tog, knit to last 3 stitches, k2tog, k1. (20 stitches)
Row 10: Purl.
Repeat rows 9 and 10 rows until 14 stitches remain.

Row 11: K1, kfb, knit to last 2 stitches, kfb, k1. (16 stitches)
Row 12: Purl.
Repeat rows 11 and 12 until you have 22 stitches.

Row 13: Knit.
Row 14: Purl.
Row 15: Knit.
Row 16: Purl.

Row 17: K1, k2tog, knit to last 3 stitches, k2tog, k1. (20 stitches)
Row 18: Purl.
Repeat rows 13 to 18 until you have 16 stitches.

Row 19: Knit.
Row 20: Purl.
Row 21: Knit.
Cast off.

Fold in half with cast on and cast off edges together and with right side out. Sew one side using mattress stitch. Sew top of head (cast on and cast off edges) neatly by going back and forth from the cast on and cast off edges under one stitch on one side and one stitch on the other side. Sew remaining side, stuffing as you go.

SHEEP LEGS (MAKE 4)

Cast on 18 stitches.

Row 1 (RS): Knit.
Row 2 (WS): Purl.
repeat rows 1 and 2 until piece measures 11.5cm (4½") from cast on edge, ending after a purl row.

Row 3: [K3, kfb] 4 times, k2. (There will now be 22 stitches)
Row 4: Purl.
Row 5: Knit.
Row 6: Purl.
Row 7: [K4, kfb] 4 times, k2. (26 stitches)
Row 8: Purl.
Row 9: Knit.
Row 10: Knit (this creates a ridge to define the bottom of the sheep's foot).
Row 11: [K2tog] 13 times. (13 stitches)
Row 12: Purl.
Row 13: [K2tog] 6 times, k1. (7 stitches)
Break yarn (leaving a long tail to sew up) and thread the tail through the live stitches using a tapestry needle.

Block. Sew up using mattress stitch, stuffing as you go. You can also use whipstitch to sew up if you prefer, but mattress stitch is a bit neater. At the top of the leg, sew the leg closed in a straight line.

SHEEP EARS (MAKE 2)

Cast on 16 stitches.

Row 1 (RS): Knit.
Row 2 (WS): Purl.
Repeat rows 1 and 2 until piece measures 6cm (2½"), ending after a purl row.

Row 3: [K2tog] 8 times. (There will now be 8 stitches)
Row 4: Purl.
Row 5: [K2tog] 4 times. (4 stitches)
Break yarn, leaving a long tail to sew up, and thread through
stitches on needle.

Block. Fold in half and sew up (do not stuff).

TO MAKE UP
Weave in ends that will not be used to attach pieces together.

Put cosy on hot water bottle.

Use the photos as a reference for the face embroidery and ear
positioning.

Sew the ears onto the stuffed head, folding or pleating at the
base of the ear to form a natural ear shape.

EMBROIDER THE NOSTRILS
Space the nostrils 8 stitches apart at the widest part at the
bottom of the head. Sew three times over two stitches for each
nostril.

EMBROIDER THE EYES
Measure down 4.5cm (1¾") from the top of the head. Space the
eyes 5 stitches apart. Sew each eye as a long straight stitch over
3 knitted stitches, and then bring the needle up slightly below
and in the middle of the long stitch. Catch the long stitch and
take the needle down again in the same hole. Repeat for the
other eye.

Put your bottle cosy on your hot water bottle. Fold down turn
over at neck if applicable.

Position head on neck of bottle and sew in place vertically (by
sewing vertically you won't affect the stretch of the rib).

Position legs at shoulders and bottom of bottle and sew in place.

Make sure you are using a blunt tapestry needle so that you
can't make a hole in your hot water bottle.

baa ram ewe LEARN TO KNIT AT HOME

ivy tea cosy

Keep your tea warm and your teapot stylish with a pom pom topped cosy knitted in a welted pattern.

YARN
Dovestone Natural Aran
Shade 7, 155m/170yds [1 skein]

NEEDLES
4.5mm (US 7) straight needles.
Plastic pom pom maker **or** cardboard circles to make a pom pom of about 7cm/2¾" diameter.

GAUGE
20 sts x 36 rows =10cm/4" in welted stitch pattern, after blocking.
Getting the right gauge is important for this pattern. If you knit too loosely or tightly your tea cosy might not come out the size specified in the pattern, and might not fit your teapot. You may need to change needle size to obtain the right gauge.

ABBREVIATIONS
A list of standard abbreviations appears on the inside back cover.

FINISHED SIZE
One size fits a medium sized teapot. Shown on a teapot 14cm (5½") tall with a 51cm (20") circumference at the base of the handle.

TEA COSY (MAKE 2 PIECES)
Cast on 38 stitches.

Row 1 (RS): Purl.
Row 2 (WS): Knit.
Row 3: Purl.
Row 4: Knit.

Row 5: Knit.
Row 6: Purl.
Row 7: Knit.
Row 8: Purl.

Repeat rows 1-8 seven more times. 64 rows worked.

Row 9: Purl.
Row 10: Knit.
Row 11: Purl.
Row 12: Knit.

Row 13: K3, k2tog, [k4, k2tog] five times, k3. (There will now be 32 stitches)
Row 14: Purl.
Row 15: Knit.
Row 16: Purl.

Row 17: Purl.

Row 18: Knit.
Row 19: Purl.
Row 20: Knit.

Row 21: [K3, k2tog] six times, k2. (26 stitches)
Row 22: Purl.
Row 23: Knit.
Row 24: Purl.

Row 25: Purl.
Row 26: Knit.
Row 27: Purl.
Row 28: Knit.

Row 29: [K2, k2tog] six times, k2. (20 stitches)
Row 30: Purl.
Row 31: Knit.
Row 32: Purl.

Row 33: Purl.
Row 34: Knit.
Row 35: Purl.

Row 36: Knit.

Row 37: [K1, k2tog] six times, k2. (14 stitches)
Row 38: Purl.
Row 39: Knit.
Row 40: Purl.

Row 41: Purl.
Row 42: Knit.

Cast off.

FINISHING

Weave in ends and block pieces following instructions on page 17.

Sew the cast off edges together. Sew up the bottom 4cm (1½") on each side. Leave a gap of about 12cm (4¾") for the spout or handle on each side and sew the rest of the seam up to the top.

Make a pompom following the instructions on page 14.

Sew the pom pom to the top of the tea cosy.

glenda mitts

Fingerless mitts are perfect for chilly days when you need a bit of extra cosiness for your hands. The welted pattern with simple thumb shaping can be scrunched up or pulled down depending on how you like to wear them.

YARN
Dovestone Natural Aran, Shade 4, 120m/131 yds [1 skein]

NEEDLES
4.5mm (US 7) straight needles.
Scrap yarn in a contrasting colour

GAUGE
20 stitches x 36 rows =10cm/4" in welted stitch pattern, after blocking.

Getting the right gauge is important for this pattern. If you knit too loosely you might run out of yarn and your mitts could be too big. If you knit too tightly your mitts might be too small to fit on your hands. You may need to change needle size to obtain the right gauge.

ABBREVIATIONS
A list of standard abbreviations appears on the inside back cover.

FINISHED SIZE
Circumference: 19cm (7½")
Length: 18cm (7")

HOW TO SLIP STITCHES TO SCRAP YARN
Thread a tapestry needle with a piece of yarn in a contrasting colour. Hold the tapestry needle in your right hand and use it to slip the required number of stitches from the left knitting needle. When you have slipped all the stitches needed to scrap yarn, you can unthread the tapestry needle. If you are worried about the scrap yarn coming out, tie the ends together.

MITTS (MAKE 2)
Cast on 38 stitches.

Row 1 (RS): Purl.
Row 2 (WS): Knit.
Row 3: Purl.
Row 4: Knit.

Row 5: Knit.
Row 6: Purl.
Row 7: Knit.
Row 8: Purl.

Repeat rows 1 to 8 once more. 16 rows worked.

Row 9: Purl.
Row 10: Knit.
Row 11: Purl.
Row 12: Knit.

Row 13: Knit.
Row 14: Purl.
Row 15: K1, [k5, kfb] 5 times, k7. (There will now be 43 stitches)
Row 16: Purl.

Row 17: Purl.
Row 18: Knit.
Row 19: Purl.
Row 20: Knit.

Row 21: Knit.
Row 22: Purl.
Row 23: K1, [k6, kfb] 5 times, k7. (48 stitches)
Row 24: Purl.

Row 25: Purl.
Row 26: Knit.
Row 27: Purl.
Row 28: Knit.

Row 29: Knit.
Row 30: Purl.
Row 31: K1, [k7, kfb] 5 times, k7. (53 stitches)
Row 32: Purl.

DIVIDE FOR THE THUMB
Row 33: P17, slip next 18 stitches to scrap yarn for the thumb, then purl the next stitch using the working yarn to create the thumbhole. Make sure you pull the yarn snug when you do this. Continue to purl to end of row. 35 stitches left on the needle
Row 34: Knit.
Row 35: Purl.
Row 36: Knit.

Row 37: Knit.
Row 38: Purl.
Row 39: Knit.
Row 40: Purl.

Row 41: Purl.
Row 42: Knit.
Row 43: Purl.
Row 44: Knit.

Repeat rows 37 to 44 twice more.

Cast off.

THUMB
Hold the mitt with the right side facing you and slip the stitches held on scrap yarn onto a knitting needle starting with the first stitch on the left. You will rejoin your yarn by working the first stitch (see instructions on page 11 for joining new yarn).

Row 1: Purl.
Row 2: Knit.
Row 3: Purl.
Row 4: Knit.

Cast off.

FINISHING
Weave in ends and block.
Sew side seam and thumb seam. Before sewing, check that you have them the right way out otherwise your mitts won't match. You can tell which is the right side by looking at the cuff of the mitt: on the right side you will see 4 rows of purl bumps.

ACKNOWLEDGEMENTS

Thank you to everyone involved in this book – it couldn't have happened without any of you:

Nic Blackmore for the fantastic layout

Rachel Brown for patient tech editing

Joelle Trousdale for gorgeous photography and all-round awesomeness

Katherine Johnson for fabulous styling

The gorgeous **Rosalyn Raine** for her wonderful modelling and her beautiful cottage in Holmfirth where we shot this book.

Our super sample knitters Jess Dyche, Rachel Hunnybun, Joelle Trousdale, Jane Brumwell, Sarah Holmes, Anne-Marie Kissoon, Sue Fenton, Sarah Burdall, Joan Banks, Andrew Iskauskas, Becky Holdsworth, Hazel Weller, Tina McAra, Helen Weir, Glenda Rodriquez

Chris Britton for schematics and diagrams

Verity, Jo and the whole team at baa ram ewe

Sirdar Spinning Ltd for permission to use the technical illustrations

LEARN TO KNIT AT HOME

First published in 2017 by baa ram ewe

Printed in Yorkshire by Wyke Printers Ltd.

British Cataloguing in Publication Data:
A catalogue record for this book is available from the British Library.

ISBN 978-0-9927730-6-9